VALERIA'S PEN

written by
Matthew Charlton

illustrated by
Monika Wnek

As the school bus rumbled along the road, the kids couldn't contain their excitement. A school trip was thrilling enough, but a trip to the zoo made this one of the best days possible.

Valeria, however, was deep in thought. She loved a school trip as much as anyone else, but there was something she loved even more:

Writing.

As part of their trip, they had to write a report on their favourite animal at the zoo, and Valeria wanted to get started right away.

She didn't even need to think about it.
She knew what her favourite animal was.
Taking out her notebook, she reached into
her pocket for a pen and –

Hang on.

There was nothing there!
It didn't make sense. Valeria always carried a pen!

It must have dropped on the floor, she thought, reaching under her seat.
And as she did so, a pen rolled out between her feet.
A fancy, golden pen.
It wasn't one she'd ever seen before, but it was just what she needed.

Opening to a fresh page in her notebook,
she began her report.
The ferocious lion walks through the grass nearby,
she wrote. A great start. This report
was going to be easy.

But just when she went to write
more, the girl next to her let
out a loud, high-pitched scream.

"*What is it?*" the teacher asked.
"*I thought I just saw... a LION!*" the girl exclaimed,
pointing to the field out of the window.
All the kids laughed.
"*Don't be silly,*" sighed the teacher.
"*Come on now, we're almost there.*"

When they arrived at the zoo,
the kids immediately ran off to find
their favourite animal. Valeria knew
exactly where she was going,
but none of her classmates could
make up their minds.

However, when Valeria
got to the lion enclosure,
she searched high and low...

But it was just no use.
She couldn't see the big cat anywhere.
Even the zookeepers couldn't find it among
the grass and trees.

Well, if the lion isn't going to show itself, Valeria
thought, *then I'm going to have to find a new
animal to write about.*

As Valeria wandered about with her notebook and pen, something suddenly echoed across the park.

Of course, she thought. *The next best thing to a lion is...*

A sea lion!

Following the sound of barking and slapping flippers, Valeria made her way to the pool.

The sea lions barked loud enough to break glass, Valeria wrote, giggling to herself. Maybe this would be even more fun than writing about lions.

But as soon as her pen left the paper, another noise rang out behind her.

The sound of breaking glass!

As Valeria turned around, glass shattered all over the floor.
A window of the penguin enclosure had cracked
and penguins were waddling out onto the path.

They had broken free!

Looking down at her notebook,
Valeria whispered the last two words.

Break glass.

It must have been a coincidence.
But then again...

Looking closely at the golden pen,
she started to wonder.
She carefully wrote another sentence.

*Suddenly, an elephant walked by and scooped up
the runaway penguins.*

Thud. Thud. Thud.

Valeria's breath caught in her throat. From around the corner, with a mighty trumpet call, a humungous elephant appeared.

In a moment, it had scooped up the little penguins and placed them neatly on its back.

So it was true.

This pen – it was magic!

Whatever she wrote down would happen in real life.

But what was she supposed to do with this power?

There was only one thing she could think of...

Just in time to save my report,
the lion appeared and saved the day! she wrote.

There, now at least she knew that her report
would be finished in time.

But just as she dotted
the full stop, a sea lion
barked out as loud as it could,
making the elephant jump in fright.

Flicking out its trunk, it knocked
into Valeria and sent her pen
flying through the air.

She watched as it landed directly
in the chimpanzee enclosure.

Before she could even blink,
a chimpanzee picked it up and looked
at it with curiosity in its eyes.

It scratched the pen on the ground, drawing strange shapes in the mud.

Valeria didn't have to guess what they were, because suddenly,
bananas appeared from thin air. The chimpanzee was using the magic pen!

Soon, there was a pile of bananas so big
that it reached as high as the enclosure wall.

Valeria tried to lean in and grab the pen,
but in one swift movement the chimpanzee
ran up the banana tower and leapt right over her.

As it disappeared into the crowds of shocked people,
Valeria saw just how much chaos she had caused.

Her teacher was running from the hungry chimpanzee.
Zookeepers were trying to surround the stomping elephant.
A waddle of penguins was marching away with the kids'
reports in their beaks.

Even if she could get the magic pen back,
Valeria had no idea what she could possibly do.

Suddenly, she saw something – a big, looming shape.
It leapt through the air and landed between her teacher
and the chimpanzee.

The lion!
It had appeared just in time!

The chimpanzee got such a fright that it dropped the pen immediately and scampered off back to its enclosure.

Without wasting a second, Valeria grabbed the pen and opened her notebook.

She was going to put an end to this, once and for all!

The animals all went straight back to their enclosures, she wrote. The glass was all fixed, everything went back to normal and everyone forgot EVERYTHING!

Valeria put a firm full stop on the page and closed her notebook with a snap.

As if by magic, the elephant stomped back to its field.

The penguins slid back into their pool.

The chimpanzee climbed back into its enclosure and the pile of bananas disappeared with a *poof!*

Then there was silence.

Valeria looked about nervously.
The glass was fixed, and the animals were back where
they belonged. Her teacher and classmates opened their
eyes wide with surprise, but then suddenly
relaxed again, as if nothing had
ever happened.

"They must have had a new
interactive show!" her teacher
said. "That was fun,
wasn't it, kids?"

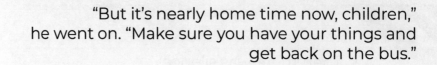

"But it's nearly home time now, children," he went on. "Make sure you have your things and get back on the bus."

But before she left, Valeria had one more thing that she needed to do.

Peering through the glass, she looked high and low and –

There it was!
The lion, prowling through the grass, right where it should be.

"I'll finish the report at home," she said
to herself. "And save this pen for when
I really need it."

Printed in Great Britain
by Amazon

28304517R00016